Here Comes Little Chimp

Story by Jenny Giles
Illustrations by Rachel Tonkin

Here is Little Chimp.

Mother Chimp is up in the tree.

"Come on, Little Chimp," said Mother Chimp. "Come up the tree to me."

"I am too little to come up the tree," said Little Chimp.

"Come on, Little Chimp,"

said Mother Chimp.

"Come up the tree."

Up, up, up,

comes Little Chimp.

Little Chimp comes

up the tree

to Mother Chimp.

Little Chimp is up in the tree.